COUNTRY PROFILES

TURKEY

BY GOLRIZ GOLKAR

BELLWETHER MEDIA • MINNEAPOLIS, MN

This edition first published in 2021 by Bellwether Media, Inc.

No part of this publication may be reproduced in whole or in part without written permission of the publisher.
For information regarding permission, write to Bellwether Media, Inc., Attention: Permissions Department,
6012 Blue Circle Drive, Minnetonka, MN 55343.

Library of Congress Cataloging-in-Publication Data

Names: Golkar, Golriz, author.
Title: Turkey / by Golriz Golkar.
Description: Minneapolis, MN : Bellwether Media, 2021. | Series: Blastoff! Discovery: Country Profiles | Includes bibliographical references and index. | Audience: Ages 7-13 | Audience: Grades 4-6 | Summary: "Engaging images accompany information about Turkey. The combination of high-interest subject matter and narrative text is intended for students in grades 3 through 8" Provided by publisher.
Identifiers: LCCN 2020049057 (print) | LCCN 2020049058 (ebook) | ISBN 9781644874523 (library binding) | ISBN 9781648341298 (ebook)
Subjects: LCSH: Turkey–Juvenile literature. | Turkey–Social life and customs–Juvenile literature.
Classification: LCC DR417.4 .G65 2021 (print) | LCC DR417.4 (ebook) | DDC 956.1–dc23
LC record available at https://lccn.loc.gov/2020049057
LC ebook record available at https://lccn.loc.gov/2020049058

Text copyright © 2021 by Bellwether Media, Inc. BLASTOFF! DISCOVERY and associated logos are trademarks and/or registered trademarks of Bellwether Media, Inc.

Editor: Kieran Downs   Designer: Josh Brink

Printed in the United States of America, North Mankato, MN.

TABLE OF CONTENTS

THE MAGIC OF ISTANBUL	4
LOCATION	6
LANDSCAPE AND CLIMATE	8
WILDLIFE	10
PEOPLE	12
COMMUNITIES	14
CUSTOMS	16
SCHOOL AND WORK	18
PLAY	20
FOOD	22
CELEBRATIONS	24
TIMELINE	26
TURKEY FACTS	28
GLOSSARY	30
TO LEARN MORE	31
INDEX	32

THE MAGIC OF ISTANBUL

THE GRAND BAZAAR

A family wanders through the gates of the Grand Bazaar of Istanbul. They gaze at the dazzling stalls of gold jewelry and colorful rugs. The smell of juicy *döner kebab* sandwiches lures them to a nearby restaurant. They enjoy their lunch with a cup of thick Turkish coffee.

ONE HUGE MARKET
The Grand Bazaar is one of the largest covered markets in the world.

OTHER TOP SITES
BLUE MOSQUE

CAPPADOCIA

EPHESUS

TOPKAPI PALACE

In the afternoon, they visit the Hagia Sophia Grand **Mosque**, Turkey's most popular location for **tourists**. Light streams through the towering dome windows, casting a glow over the glittering gold **mosaics**. They marvel at the ancient **architecture**. Turkey is a country of both old and new treasures!

LOCATION

ONE CITY, TWO CONTINENTS
Istanbul is one of the few cities in the world to span two continents. Its west bank lies in Europe while its east bank lies in Asia.

Turkey connects Europe and Asia. It covers 302,535 square miles (783,562 square kilometers) of the **Middle East**. Most of the country is in Asia. The northwestern area, Thrace, lies in southeastern Europe.

The Black Sea borders Turkey to the north. Bulgaria and Greece border Turkey to the northwest. The Aegean Sea and the Marmara Sea lap against Turkey's western coast. The Mediterranean Sea washes on the southern coast. Syria and Iraq lie to the southeast. Iran, Azerbaijan, Armenia, and Georgia border on the east and northeast. The capital, Ankara, is located in the northwest. Turkey also includes 500 islands.

LANDSCAPE AND CLIMATE

Turkey is mostly mountainous. The Pontic Mountains stretch across the north. In the east, high mountains peak at Mount Ararat. The Tigris and Euphrates Rivers also start in eastern Turkey. Southeastern Turkey is covered by a **massif** called the Arabian platform. In the west, coastal **plains** extend toward a large central **plateau**. In the northwest, the Bosporus and Dardanelles **Straits** connect the Black Sea and the Aegean Sea.

PONTIC MOUNTAINS

EUPHRATES RIVER

ANKARA
Average seasonal highs and lows

JANUARY
HIGH: 38 °F (3 °C)
LOW: 24 °F (-4 °C)

APRIL
HIGH: 61 °F (16 °C)
LOW: 39 °F (4 °C)

JULY
HIGH: 85 °F (29 °C)
LOW: 59 °F (15 °C)

OCTOBER
HIGH: 66 °F (19 °C)
LOW: 41 °F (5 °C)

°F = degrees Fahrenheit
°C = degrees Celsius

EARTHQUAKE!
Turkey lies in a region that experiences more earthquakes than most other places in the world.

Turkey's coastal regions have a Mediterranean climate. Summers are hot and dry, while winters are cool and wet. The inland plateau has little rainfall and large seasonal changes. Mountainous areas receive more rain and snow.

WILDLIFE

GRAY WOLF

Turkey is home to many animals. Eurasian lynxes and brown bears quietly roam the forests. Gray wolves, the national animal, hunt chamois in the mountains. White-throated robins chatter from their nests high up in the mountains. Black vultures and Eurasian sparrowhawks soar above, looking for animal scraps.

WHITE-THROATED ROBIN

Mediterranean monk seals and loggerhead turtles swim in the warm Mediterranean and Aegean waters. They feast on crabs, striped red mullet, and sharpsnout sea bream that splash about. Harbor porpoises eat anchovies in the Black Sea.

MEDITERRANEAN MONK SEAL

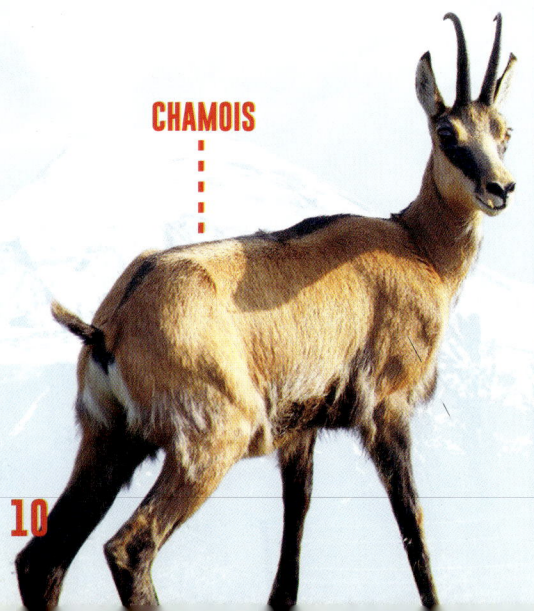
CHAMOIS

BLACK VULTURE

EURASIAN LYNX

EURASIAN LYNX

Life Span: up to 17 years
Red List Status: least concern

Eurasian lynx range =

| LEAST CONCERN | NEAR THREATENED | VULNERABLE | ENDANGERED | CRITICALLY ENDANGERED | EXTINCT IN THE WILD | EXTINCT |

11

PEOPLE

RELIGIOUS FREEDOM
While nearly the entire Turkish population practices Islam, the country does not have an official state religion. People are free to practice any religion they want.

More than 82 million people live in Turkey. About 7 out of 10 have Turkish roots. About 1 out of 5 people are Kurdish, making up the second-largest **ethnic** group in the country. Greek, Jewish, and Armenian communities are found in Istanbul. Georgian, Circassian, and Laz populations live in the east.

Most Turks are Sunni Muslims. Other Muslim Turks practice Alevi beliefs, which combine Islam with elements of Turkish **culture**. Christianity and Judaism are also practiced in Turkey. The official language of the country is Turkish.

FAMOUS FACE
Name: Mehmet Okur
Birthday: May 26, 1979
Hometown: Yalova, Turkey
Famous for: Former NBA All-Star and the first NBA coach of Turkish descent

ISTANBUL

SPEAK TURKISH

ENGLISH	TURKISH	HOW TO SAY IT
hello	merhaba	mehr-HAH-bah
goodbye	güle güle	goo-LAY goo-LAY
please	lütfen	LEWT-fehn
thank you	teşekkür ederim	TESH-ek-kewr eh-DEHR-ehm
yes	evet	ay-VEHT
no	hayır	hi-EHR

COMMUNITIES

Most Turks live in **urban** areas. City dwellers often live in apartments. Wealthy Turks may live in single-family homes and townhouses in the **suburbs**. Taxis, buses, and subways provide transportation. The underwater Marmaray Tunnel connects the Asian and European sides of Istanbul.

ISTANBUL

HOME SWEET HOME
Turks consider owning a home to be a sign of success. If they can afford it, Turkish parents buy a home for each of their children to give them in the future.

Rural Turks live in small homes made from concrete or brick. Inside, the homes are decorated with **traditional** art and carpets. Most houses only have one or two rooms. The whole family may sleep in the living room. Minibuses called *dolmuş* transport people within and between towns and villages. Trains are used for traveling longer distances.

CUSTOMS

Turks are very friendly. They often invite friends and family to their homes. Guests remove their shoes before entering a home. Hosts serve refreshments such as tea and Turkish sweets. Tea is also served to customers in shops.

Some Turks believe in keeping away the bad luck of the evil eye. Anything valuable needs to be protected from jealous looks. To keep negative energy away, small glass decorations in the shape of blue eyes called *nazar boncuğu* are hung above doors in homes and shops. They are even pinned to newborn babies and worn as jewelry.

NAZAR BONCUĞU

SCHOOL AND WORK

Turkish children must attend school from ages 5 to 18. Elementary, middle, and high school last for four years each. Middle school students study for exams to get in to high schools. After high school graduation, students may attend universities or trade schools.

About half of the Turkish population holds a **service job**. These include tourism or office jobs. **Manufacturing** workers may work in **textile**, steel, or food processing factories. In rural areas, Turks may work on farms that grow cotton or fruits. All over the country, craftspeople work in skilled trades such as weaving, jewelry making, and carpentry.

RESTAURANT WORKER

WEAVING

PLAY

SOCCER

Turks enjoy playing and watching soccer. They support many regional teams and the national team. Water sports such as swimming, kitesurfing, and paragliding are popular along the coasts. Turks enjoy skiing in the northwest. Turkey's national sport is oil wrestling. Wrestlers covered in olive oil compete for up to 40 minutes. The wrestler who is pinned down on his back loses the match.

OIL WRESTLING

During their free time, Turks visit friends and enjoy picnics with family. Games are very popular in Turkey. Good backgammon players often earn respect. Chess, checkers, and card games are also popular.

BACKGAMMON

EBRU

Ebru is a Turkish art form that creates beautiful marbled patterns. Create your own Turkish masterpiece by following these easy steps!

What You Need:
- one can of shaving cream
- several colors of acrylic paint
- one baking sheet
- popsicle sticks
- a butter knife
- cardstock or watercolor paper

What You Do:
1. Cover the baking sheet with shaving cream and smooth the shaving cream with a popsicle stick.
2. Squeeze different colors of paint onto the shaving cream, making dots and lines.
3. With another popsicle stick, swirl the paint to make a design you like.
4. Take a piece of cardstock or watercolor paper, and gently press it over the design.
5. Remove the paper, and let it dry for a minute.
6. When the shaving cream is nearly dry, gently scrape off the shaving cream with a butter knife.
7. Let the paper dry completely.
8. Hang your artwork, or use it as a greeting card.

FOOD

KAHVE

Turkish breakfasts consist of bread with white cheese, butter, and honey. For lunch, beef or lamb *kebabs* are eaten *Adana* style with spices or *Beyti* style wrapped in thin bread. Vegetables and *pilaf* rice are eaten on the side. Puddings and *baklava* pastries are popular desserts. Strong coffee called *kahve* is usually enjoyed at every meal.

Dinner is often the main meal of the day. It may begin with *meze* dishes such as stuffed grape leaves, sardine salad, or garlic yogurt. A main course such as *kuzu tandır*, a lamb dish, may be served next. Coastal regions serve fish such as roasted sea bass.

MEZE DISHES

KUZU TANDIR

KEŞKÜL

This creamy pudding is a favorite Turkish dessert! Have an adult help you make this tasty recipe.

Ingredients:
1 cup sugar
3 egg yolks
1 1/2 tablespoons rice flour
1 1/2 tablespoons cornstarch
4 cups milk
1/2 cup peeled and crushed almonds
1/2 tablespoon vanilla
1/2 cup cream
1/2 cup peeled and crushed almonds
pistachios, raisins, and almonds for topping

Steps:
1. Place the sugar and egg yolks in a medium-sized pot.
2. Pour rice flour, cornstarch, and 1/4 cup milk into a medium-sized bowl and mix. Set aside.
3. Add the remaining milk to the pot and beat again. Place the pot over high heat, and bring the ingredients to a boil, stirring from time to time. Add the rice flour and cornstarch mixture, and stir for three minutes.
4. Add the crushed almonds, vanilla, and cream. Keep stirring.
5. When the pudding has thickened, remove from heat. It should have a creamy texture.
6. Serve the pudding in small cups, and allow it to cool in the cups at room temperature.
7. When the pudding has cooled, decorate with the pistachio, raisin, and almond topping and serve.

CELEBRATIONS

Most Turks observe Muslim holidays. They **fast** from dawn until sundown every year during the holy month of Ramadan. When fasting ends, they celebrate with loved ones for three days during Şeker Bayramı.

Turks also celebrate state holidays. April 23 is Children's Day and the date when the Turkish government was established. One Turkish child is chosen to assist the president that day. Military parades and music mark the occasion. Children celebrate with candy and dancing. Republic Day is celebrated on October 29. It celebrates the start of the Turkish Republic with concerts and parades. Turks are proud of their culture and traditions!

CHILDREN'S DAY

SANTA CLAUS IS COMING TO TOWN

Saint Nicholas was born in present-day Patara, Turkey, around 300 CE. Tales of his generosity became known all over the world, leading the Dutch to name him Sinterklaas. Today, he is often called Santa Claus.

WAITING FOR SUNSET DURING RAMADAN

TIMELINE

330 CE
Emperor Constantine I makes Constantinople (present-day Istanbul) the capital of the Roman Empire

1928
Turkey becomes a secular state, giving inhabitants freedom of religion

1984
The Kurds begin fighting for independence

1453
Ottoman Turks take over Constantinople, making the Balkans and Asia Minor part of the Ottoman Empire

1960
The Turkish military takes over the democratic government, ruling the country on and off for the next 23 years

1923
Turkey becomes an independent republic with Kemal Atatürk as the first president

2002
Turkish women are granted full legal equality with men

2014
Erdogan wins the first direct popular presidential election

2007
Thousands of protesters gather in Ankara to pressure Prime Minister Erdogan to drop out of the presidential race due to his Islamist background

2019
The United States removes troops from war-torn northern Syria, leading to Turkey attacking the United States's Kurdish allies in the area

TURKEY FACTS

Official Name: Republic of Turkey

Flag: The Turkish flag is red with a white crescent moon close to the center and a white five-pointed star to the right of the moon. These symbols represent the various ethnic groups in Turkey. It is believed that the flag stands for the reflection of the moon and a star in Turkish warriors' pools of blood.

Area: 302,535 square miles (783,562 square kilometers)

Capital City: Ankara

Important Cities: Istanbul, Izmir, Bursa, Adana

Population: 82,017,514 (July 2020)

WHERE PEOPLE LIVE
COUNTRYSIDE 23.9%
CITY 76.1%

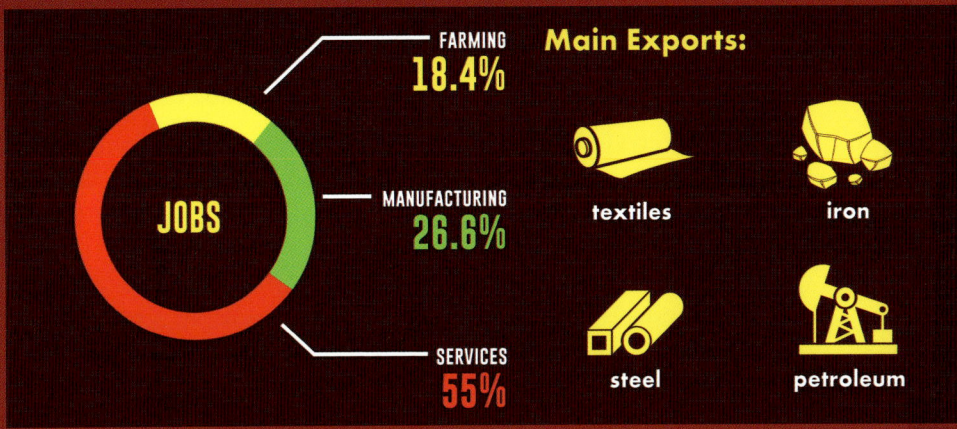

National Holiday:
Republic Day (October 29)

Main Languages:
Turkish (official), Kurdish

Form of Government:
presidential republic

Title for Country Leader:
president

Unit of Money:
Turkish lira

GLOSSARY

architecture—the design of buildings

culture—the beliefs, arts, and ways of life in a place or society

ethnic—related to a group of people who share customs and an identity

fast—to stop eating all foods or particular foods for a time

manufacturing—a field of work in which people use machines to make products

massif—a tightly packed group of mountains

Middle East—a region of southwestern Asia and northern Africa; this region includes Egypt, Lebanon, Iran, Iraq, Israel, Saudi Arabia, Turkey, and other nearby countries.

mosaics—images or patterns made up of small colored pieces

mosque—a building that Muslims use for worship

plains—large areas of flat land

plateau—an area of flat, raised land

rural—related to the countryside

service job—a job that performs a task for a person or business

straits—narrow channels connecting two large bodies of water

suburbs—towns and communities just outside of a large city

textile—a fabric that is woven or knit

tourists—people who travel to visit another place

traditional—related to customs, ideas, or beliefs handed down from one generation to the next

urban—related to cities and city life

TO LEARN MORE

AT THE LIBRARY

Klepeis, Alicia Z. *Iran*. Minneapolis, Minn.: Bellwether Media, 2020.

Mattern, Joanne. *Turkey*. New York, N.Y.: Cavendish Square Publishing, 2018.

Murray, Julie. *Turkey*. Minneapolis, Minn.: Abdo Publishing, 2015.

ON THE WEB

Factsurfer.com gives you a safe, fun way to find more information.

1. Go to www.factsurfer.com.

2. Enter "Turkey" into the search box and click 🔍.

3. Select your book cover to see a list of related content.

INDEX

activities, 21
Ankara, 6, 7, 9
capital (see Ankara)
celebrations, 24-25
Children's Day, 24
climate, 9
communities, 14-15
customs, 16-17
ebru (activity), 21
education, 18
fast facts, 28-29
food, 4, 16, 22-23
housing, 14, 15
Istanbul, 4-5, 6, 12, 13, 14
landmarks, 4, 5
landscape, 8-9, 10
language, 13
location, 6-7
Okur, Mehmet, 13

people, 12-13
Ramadan, 24, 25
recipe, 23
religion, 12, 13, 24
Republic Day, 24
Saint Nicholas, 25
Şeker Bayramı, 24
size, 7
sports, 20
timeline, 26-27
transportation, 14, 15
wildlife, 10-11
work, 19

The images in this book are reproduced through the courtesy of: Boris Stroujko, front cover, pp. 4-5; Yarygin, p. 5 (Blue Mosque); Punnawit Suwattananun, p. 5 (Cappadocia); muratart, p. 5 (Ephesus); Ruslan Kalnitsky, p. 5 (Topkapi Palace); Dmitri Kalvan, p. 8; Funtay, p. 9; BilalKocabas, p. 9 (Ankara); Real PIX, p. 10 (chamois); Bildagentur Zoonar GmbH, p. 10 (gray wolf)(Eurasian lynx); Andre Valadao, p. 10 (white-throated robin); zaferkizilkaya, p. 10 (Mediterranean monk seal); MehmetO, p. 12; Joe Giddens/ Alamy, p. 13 (Mehmet Okur); MDart10, p. 13; Murat Can Kirmizigul, p. 14; Preisler, p. 15; Pascal Mannaerts/ Alamy, p. 16; Graca Victoria/ Alamy, p. 17; janine wiedel/ Alamy, p. 18; Ayhan Altun/ Alamy, p. 19 (restaurant worker); Katja Kreder/ Alamy, p. 19 (weaving); Basel, Switzerland, p. 20 (soccer); Mustafa Olgun/ Alamy, p. 20 (oil wrestling); LizCoughlan/ Alamy, p. 21 (backgammon); Marina Nozhko, p. 21; Images&Stories/ Alamy, p. 22; MikeDotta/ Alamy, p. 23 (meze dishes); Fanfo, p. 23 (kuzu tandir); Esin Deniz, p. 23; Yavuz Meyveci, p. 23 (Children's Day); epic_images/ Alamy, pp. 24-25; anDagnall Computing/ Alamy, p. 25 (Constantine); Sylvia Buchoolz/ Alamy, p. 27 (bottom); 360b, p. 27 (top); nexus 7, p. 29 (coin); daphnusia, p. 29 (dollar bill).